THE HISTORY OF THE ARIZONA CARDINALS

THE HISTORY OF THE ARIZONA

Published by Creative Education
123 South Broad Street
Mankato, Minnesota 56001
Creative Education is an imprint of The Creative Company.

DESIGN AND PRODUCTION BY **EVANSDAY DESIGN**

Printed in the United States of America

LIBRARY OF CONGRESS CATALOGING-IN-PUBLICATION DATA

Gilbert, Sara.
The history of the Arizona Cardinals / by Sara Gilbert.
p. cm. — (NFL today)
Summary: Traces the history of the team from its beginnings through 2003.
ISBN 1-58341-286-7
1. Arizona Cardinals (Football team)—History—Juvenile literature. [1. Arizona Cardinals (Football team)—History. 2. Football—History.] I. Title. II. Series.

GV956.A75F74 2004
796.332'64'0979173—dc22 2003065044

First edition

9 8 7 6 5 4 3 2 1

COVER PHOTO: wide receiver Anquan Boldin

PHOTOGRAPHS BY
AP/Wide World Photos, Corbis (Michael Ainsworth/Dallas Morning News, Bettmann, Rebecca Cook/Reuters), Getty Images

CARDINALS

BUILT ATOP THE RUINS OF AN OLD NATIVE AMERICAN COMMUNITY, PHOENIX, ARIZONA, WAS NAMED BY AN EARLY EXPLORER FOR THE MYTHICAL BIRD THAT BURNED UP BUT WAS REBORN FROM ITS OWN ASHES. THE DESERT CITY HAS INDEED RISEN OUT OF THOSE RUINS TO BECOME A THRIVING METROPOLITAN AREA—THE SIXTH-LARGEST CITY IN THE UNITED STATES—AND IS TODAY KNOWN FOR ITS BEAUTIFUL GOLF COURSES, NATIVE AMERICAN HISTORY, AND REJUVENATING CLIMATE. PHOENIX IS ALSO KNOWN AS A HOT SPOT FOR SPORTS FANS, BEING ONE OF EIGHT AMERICAN CITIES WITH TEAMS IN ALL FOUR MAJOR PROFESSIONAL SPORTS. ONE OF THOSE TEAMS IS CALLED THE ARIZONA CARDINALS. THE CARDINALS, WHO MOVED TO ARIZONA IN 1988, WERE FOUNDED IN 1898 AND BOAST ONE OF THE LONGEST HISTORIES IN THE NATIONAL FOOTBALL LEAGUE (NFL). AND ALTHOUGH THAT HISTORY HAS NOT BEEN FLUSH WITH SUCCESS, THE TEAM HAS LONG FOUND A PLACE IN THE HEARTS OF FANS AROUND THE COUNTRY.

[1956 Chicago Cardinals]

A CHICAGO-STYLE START>

THE CARDINALS FRANCHISE was born in Chicago, Illinois, in 1898 as the Morgan Athletic Club. The team became known as the Normals when its playing site moved to nearby Normal Field. But when team owner Chris O'Brien got a bargain on used maroon jerseys from the University of Chicago, the club changed its name again. "That's not maroon, it's Cardinal red!" O'Brien declared as his players put on the jerseys. The name hasn't changed since.

When the American Professional Football League, a forerunner of the NFL, started up in 1920, the Chicago Cardinals jumped at the chance to join. So did a cross-town club called the Tigers. O'Brien challenged the Tigers to a game, with only the winner earning the right to stay in the league. The Cardinals won that game thanks to John "Paddy" Driscoll, who scored the only touchdown of the game.

A rugged fullback and kicker, Ernie Nevers was an almost unstoppable force in the late 1920s.

Driscoll, who played running back, cornerback, and kicker, served for two seasons as the team's head coach and made the Cardinals one of the top teams in the newly created NFL. In 1925, Chicago captured its first NFL championship with an 11–2–1 record. But by then there was another team in town: the Bears. Chicago fans fell in love with the Bears, and few fans turned out to attend Cardinals games. In 1929, money problems forced O'Brien to sell his team to a Chicago doctor named David Jones.

Jones's first move as team owner was to sign Ernie Nevers, a sensational running back who had starred at Stanford University. It didn't take long for Nevers to make a name for himself in the NFL. When the Cardinals met the Bears on November 28, 1929, Nevers turned the much-anticipated matchup into a one-man show. He scored every Cardinals point in a 40–6 victory, rushing for six touchdowns, kicking four extra points, and setting an NFL single-game scoring record that still stands. When asked about the game, legendary Bears coach George Halas said, "The final score: Bears 6, Nevers 40."

Like Nevers, Ollie Matson was a versatile star, excelling at running the ball and returning kicks.

Despite the fine play of guard Walt Kiesling, the Cardinals started on a downward spiral after Nevers retired in 1932. The team did not post a winning record again until it finished 6–4–2 in 1935. World War II hit the team hard, as many of Chicago's top players—including quarterback/running back Johnny Clement, end Billy Dewell, and guard Joe Kuharich—joined the service. The Cardinals suffered eight straight losing seasons in the 1930s and '40s, including one in which they couldn't muster even one win.

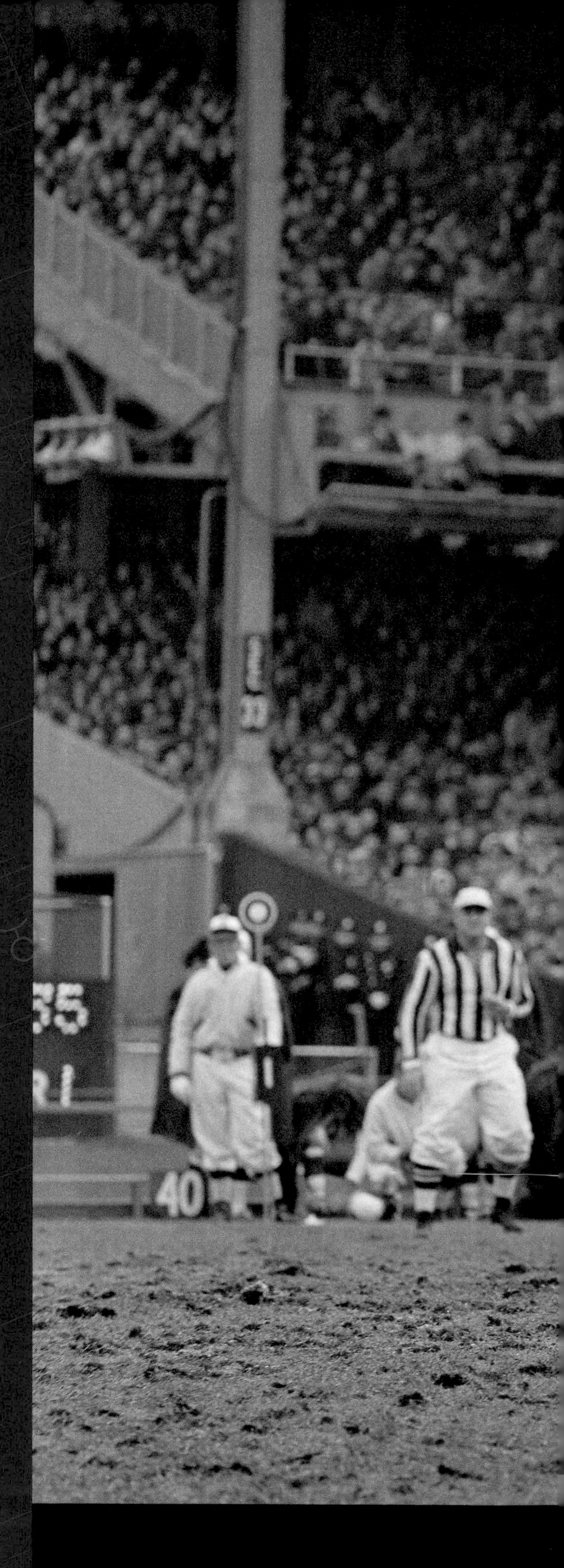

Charley Johnson (pictured) followed in the footsteps of Johnny Clement as a superb Cardinals quarterback

THE DREAM BACKFIELD>

THE CARDINALS' SLOW rise back to power actually began in 1932, when a former Chicago Bears team official named Charles W. Bidwell bought the team. Although it was all he could do to keep the team afloat during the difficult years of the 1930s, Bidwell bided his time until he could build another winning club.

The pieces began coming together when Bidwell re-hired coach Jimmy Conzelman, who had led the Cardinals from 1940 to 1942. When he came back in 1946, Coach Conzelman demanded a better pool of talent with which to work—specifically, a "Dream Backfield" made up of the best runners and passers in the league.

Bidwell spent the money necessary to get such players. Quarterback Paul Christman, fullback Pat Harder, and halfback Elmer Angsman were in place by 1946. The addition of speedy young halfback Charley Trippi in 1947 completed the backfield. Trippi was courted by many teams but signed with the Cardinals after Bidwell offered him a contract for the unheard-of sum of $100,000.

Halfback Elmer Angsman starred at famous Notre Dame University before joining Chicago in 1946

The 1947 Cardinals put together a 9–3 record, winning the NFL Western Division title and earning a shot at the league championship. Chicago jumped out to an early lead in the championship game against the Philadelphia Eagles, but the Eagles fought back. With the clock winding down, the Cardinals clung to a 28–21 lead as the Eagles marched down the field. Veteran Cardinals defensive back Marshall "Biggie" Goldberg then intercepted a pass from Philadelphia quarterback Tommy Thompson, sealing the Cardinals' second NFL championship.

The Cardinals enjoyed another winning season in 1948, compiling an 11–1 record that still stands as the best in team history. Chicago again took on Philadelphia in the title game, but this time the Eagles came out on top, 7–0. Coach Conzelman left the Cardinals after that. Although most of the pieces of his Dream Backfield remained intact, the team seemed lost without its leader, and another string of losing seasons followed.

One of the few bright spots for the Cardinals in the 1950s was a track star named Ollie Matson, who joined the team as a running back in 1952. The blazing-fast Matson could run, receive, and return kicks, but he couldn't carry the team alone. When the Los Angeles Rams offered nine players to the Cardinals in 1959 for Matson, he was traded away.

"Dream Backfield" standout Charley Trippi scored two touchdowns in the 1947 NFL championship game

MEET THEM IN ST. LOUIS>

SOON AFTER MATSON left Chicago, so did the Cardinals. Tired of seeing their team play second fiddle to the Bears, the Bidwell family moved the Cardinals to St. Louis, Missouri, in 1960. There the Cardinals began to win more fans and games, starting out with a 6–5–1 season in 1960. With fleet-footed running back John David Crow setting new team rushing records, and with wide receiver Sonny Randle emerging as one of the NFL's most electrifying scorers, the team settled into a winning groove that would last for most of the decade.

Things really began to heat up in 1966, when the Cardinals signed an unknown quarterback named Jim Hart. Little did Cardinals fans know that Hart would play 18 seasons in St. Louis and set most of the team's

In a Cardinals career that stretched from the 1960s to the '80s, Jim Hart set almost every team passing record

Known for his explosive speed, Terry Metcalf was the team's best kick returner since Ollie Matson.

passing records. In the seasons that followed, the team built a formidable offense around Hart, speedy wide receiver Mel Gray, halfback Terry Metcalf, and an offensive line that included mountainous tackle Dan Dierdorf and feared guard Conrad Dobler. In 1974, St. Louis fans cheered as the Cardinals went 10–4 and won the National Football Conference (NFC) Eastern Division title.

Although the Minnesota Vikings defeated the Cardinals in the first round of the playoffs after that 1974 season, St. Louis players and fans believed the franchise had turned the corner. "It was the first taste any of us has ever had about what's really happening in this game," said defensive end Council Rudolph. "We're young. We'll be back."

The Cardinals were back, winning the division again in 1975, but the Los Angeles Rams ousted them in the first round of the playoffs. In 1976, St. Louis went 10–4, just missing the postseason. Then, in 1977, things started to go downhill. Despite the best efforts of Pro Bowl running back Ottis Anderson, the Cardinals again fell to the bottom of the NFC standings.

GREEN AND LOMAX LEAD THE WAY>

IT WAS 1983 before the Cardinals again put together a winning record. That success was due in large part to Roy Green, a cornerback selected in the 1979 NFL Draft. Green was blessed with incredible speed, which gave Cardinals coach Jim Hanifan hope of replacing the departed Mel Gray. In 1981, Coach Hanifan took Green aside and asked him to take on additional duties as a wide receiver. "I just want you to go in and run by everybody," Hanifan explained.

Green did just that. No matter what play was called in the huddle, Green almost always had the same assignment: run deep and get open. The Cardinals considered him their secret weapon, but the secret was out the first time Green took the field on offense. In that game, Green

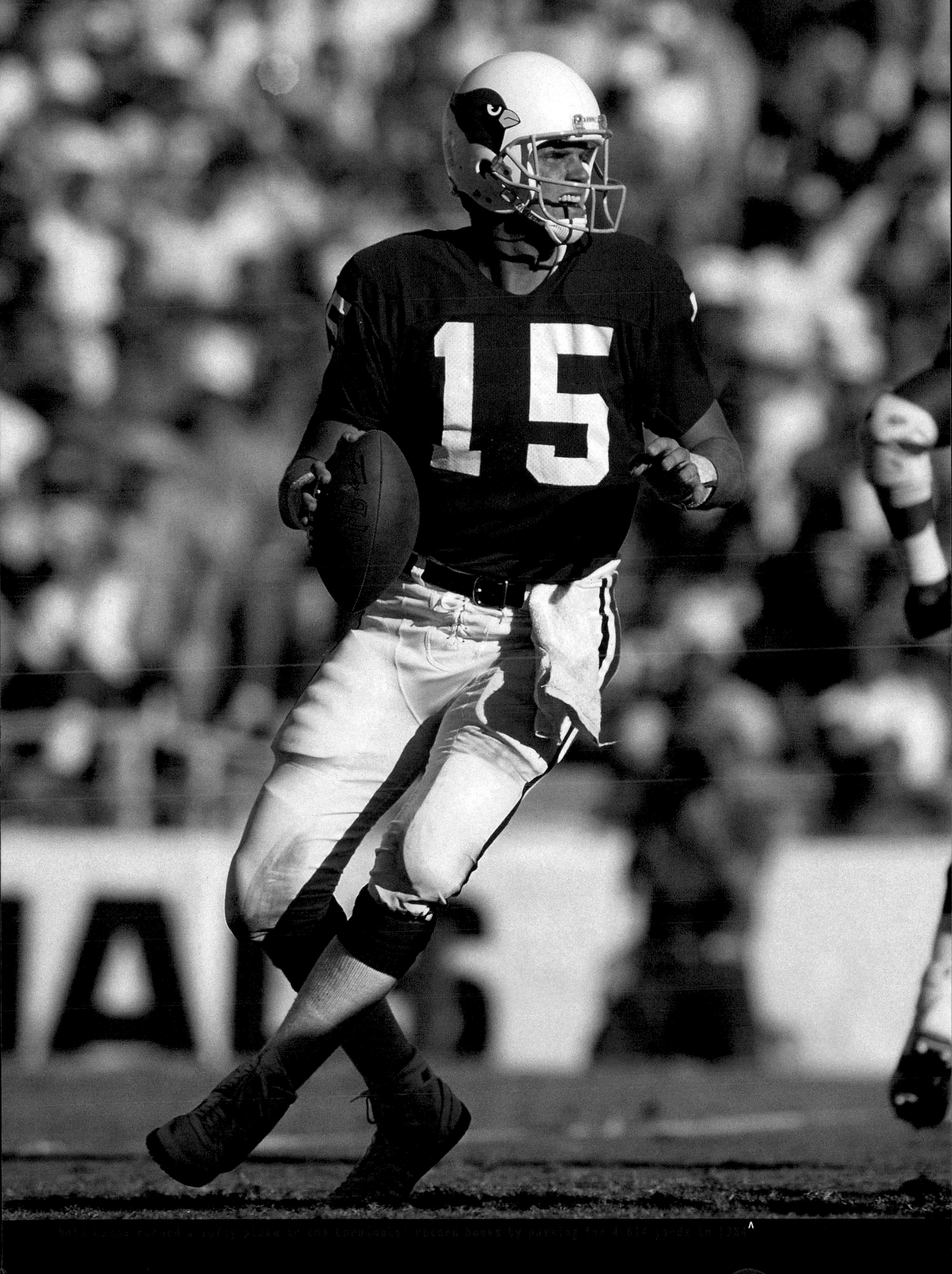

Neil Lomax earned a lofty place in the Cardinals' record books by passing for 4,614 yards in 1984

Speedster Roy Green put on some amazing shows in front of sparse home crowds during the mid-1980s.

caught a 60-yard bomb from Jim Hart. It was the first of more than 500 passes that Green would catch in his career. His 66 total touchdown receptions still stand as the team record, as do his 8,497 receiving yards.

Green became even more dangerous when quarterback Neil Lomax took over late in the 1981 season. Lomax and Green led the Cardinals to the playoffs during the strike-shortened 1982 season. The two then hooked up for 1,227 yards and 14 touchdowns in 1983. St. Louis put together winning records in 1983 and 1984 but missed the playoffs both years.

The Cardinals appeared ready for better things in 1985, but injuries to their three offensive stars—Lomax, Green, and Anderson—resulted in a disappointing season. As the Cardinals continued to struggle the next two seasons, St. Louis fans weren't willing to suffer with them. In 1987, the team played its home games in a half-filled stadium. Team owner William Bidwell, the son of the late Charles Bidwell, started looking for sunnier skies under which to play.

ON TO ARIZONA>

BIDWELL FOUND HIS sunny skies in Phoenix, Arizona, where the team moved in early 1988. Lomax gave the club's new fans something to cheer about as he bounced back from his injuries to pass for more than 3,400 yards in his first 11 games that season. Green and wide receiver J.T. Smith also put on some great shows in front of their new home crowd. But injuries then sidelined Lomax again; he would retire after missing the entire 1989 season. Green's career ended a year later. Without these leaders, the Cardinals fell into a five-year tailspin.

The Cardinals went a respectable 8–8 in 1994, then continued rebuilding in the seasons that followed. The defense featured such solid players as tackle Eric Swann and cornerback Aeneas Williams, but coach Vince Tobin

A two-time Pro Bowler, hard-charging defensive tackle Eric Swann spent nine seasons in Arizona.

knew that the offense needed a spark. In the 1997 NFL Draft, the Cardinals tried to add that spark by selecting quarterback Jake Plummer from local Arizona State University.

Known as Jake "the Snake," Plummer had won Arizona football fans over by leading the Sun Devils to an undefeated season in 1996 and a berth in the Rose Bowl. "He can make you miss, even three feet away from you," said St. Louis Rams coach Dick Vermeil. "And if you leave your feet to try to rush him, you're making a mistake because he'll duck under you, dart around, and then refocus down the field and throw a touchdown."

In 1998, Plummer delighted fans by leading the Cardinals to a 9–7 record and their first playoff appearance since 1982. The team then earned its first playoff victory in 51 years by demolishing the rival Dallas Cowboys 20–7. Although the team lost to the Minnesota Vikings the following week, hope had been restored in Arizona.

Unfortunately, that success was fleeting. The Cardinals returned to their losing ways the next two seasons despite the best efforts of Williams and linebacker Ronald McKinnon. Halfway through the 2000 season, Coach Tobin was replaced by defensive coordinator Dave McGinnis. The team's shake-up continued after the 2002 season when

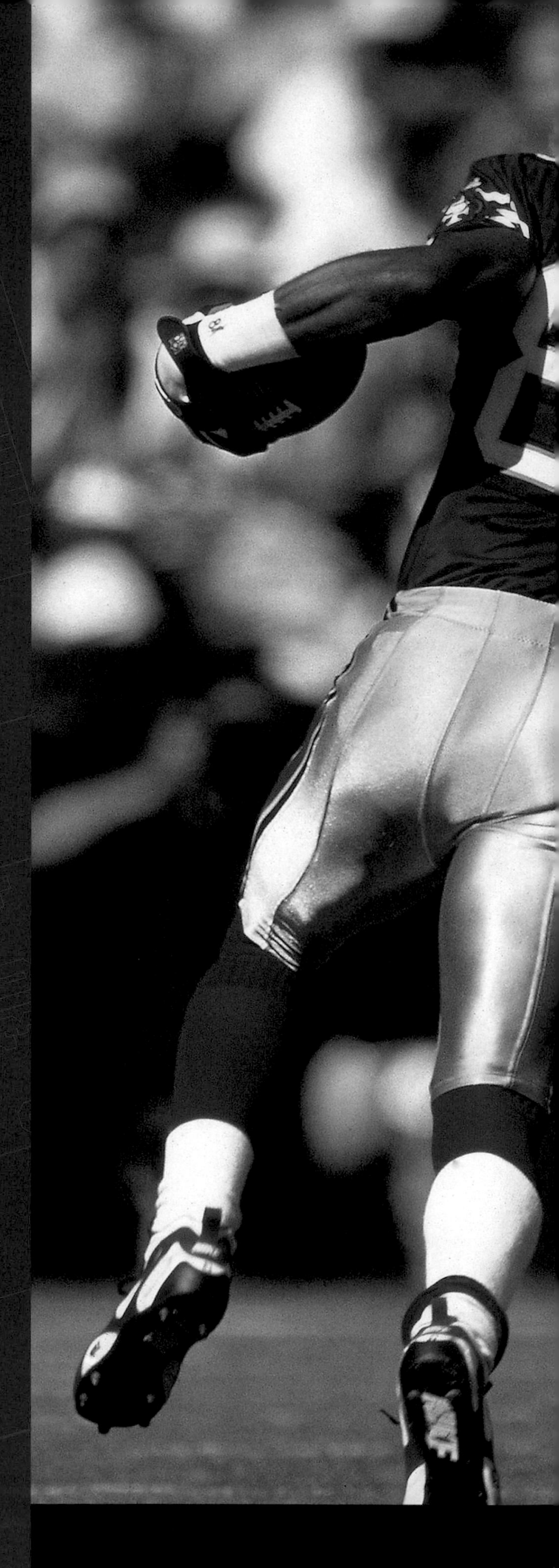

Aeneas Williams's great speed and instincts made him one of the NFL's top "shut-down" cornerbacks.

Jake Plummer thrilled Cardinals fans by leading Arizona to a long-awaited playoff victory in 1998

Plummer—who had led the team to only one winning record in five seasons—left town.

Although many Arizona fans were disappointed to see Plummer go, they were encouraged by the 2003 signing of running back Emmitt Smith, the NFL's all-time leader in rushing yards and touchdowns. Although Smith was 33 years old, the Cardinals believed the future Hall-of-Famer still had some great performances in him. With Smith lined up behind quarterback Josh McCown and alongside brilliant young receiver Anquan Boldin—all under the leadership of new coach Dennis Green—Arizona hoped to soon make some noise in the NFC Western Division.

With a history that stretches back more than a century and includes stays in three cities, the Cardinals have experienced the highest highs and lowest lows of professional football. The team has spent more than its share of seasons near the bottom of the standings, but it has also captured two world championships. As each new season begins in Arizona, fans continue to believe that the Cardinals will rise from the ashes to find championship glory once again.

Anquan Boldin earned 2003 Rookie of the Year honors

Arizona looked to Emmitt Smith for veteran leadership

Standouts such as linebacker Ronald McKinnon hoped to carry the proud Cardinals franchise back to glory ^

INDEX>